PLÁCIDO DOMINGO
Opera Superstar

David Goodnough

Enslow Publishers, Inc.
40 Industrial Road   PO Box 38
Box 398   Aldershot
Berkeley Heights, NJ 07922   Hants GU12 6BP
USA   UK
http://www.enslow.com

Library of Congress Cataloging-in-Publication Data

Goodnough, David.
    Plácido Domingo: opera superstar / David Goodnough.
        p. cm. — (Hispanic biographies)
    Includes bibliographical references and index.
    ISBN 0-89490-892-8
    1. Domingo, Plácido, 1941– . 2. Tenors (Singers)—Biography—
    Juvenile literature. I. Title. II. Series.
    ML3930.D6G66   1997
    782.1'092—dc21
    [B]   96-46451
                                              CIP
                                             MN

Permission to use excerpts from Plácido Domingo's *My First Forty Years* was
cordially granted by Weidenfeld and Nicolson Ltd.

Printed in the United States of America

10 9 8 7 6 5 4 3 2

Illustration Credits: Winnie Klotz, pp. 7, 10, 49, 51, 56, 63, 66,
77, 79, 93; AP/Wide World Photos, pp. 16, 35; Courtesy of the
Maryknoll Photo Library, p. 42; New York Public Library at Lincoln
Center, pp. 68, 73; Library for the Performing Arts, p. 25.

Cover Illustration: Library for the Performing Arts

CONTENTS

TENOR OF
RECORD

On the afternoon of Saturday, April 22, 1995, the gold curtain went up at the Metropolitan Opera House in New York City. The performance that day was of *Parsifal*, by the German composer Richard Wagner. *Parsifal* is the story of a knight's journey to find the Holy Grail, the cup from which Jesus Christ drank at the Last Supper. It is one of the longest and most difficult of all operas to perform, and it is especially demanding of the lead singer, the tenor who plays Parsifal. On this afternoon, the part was played and sung by Plácido Domingo, whom many music lovers consider to have the greatest tenor voice in the world. The opera, because of its great length, began at noon, and it was not over until 5:30 in the evening. At the end of the opera, Plácido Domingo was greeted with thunderous applause from the standing-room-only audience.

Two and a half hours later, at 8:00 P.M., the same Plácido Domingo took his place in the pit, facing the orchestra before which he had sung that afternoon. He was there to conduct the musicians and singers on stage in a performance of *Madama Butterfly*, by the Italian composer Giacomo Puccini. *Madama Butterfly* is a much different opera from *Parsifal*. It is the story of a young and innocent Japanese woman who falls in love with an American naval officer and kills herself after he has abandoned her and their child. Despite its tragic ending, it is one of the most popular operas in the world. Plácido Domingo had sung the part of Lieutenant Pinkerton, the unfaithful naval officer, many times, but for this performance, he was in charge of the whole production. At 11:00 P.M., Plácido Domingo's working day ended when he took his bows with the singers at the conclusion of the three-act opera. For the second time that day, he received an ovation from the overflow audience, which contained many people who had attended both performances. They knew that something special was happening.

Plácido Domingo stars as Parsifal, the weary knight, in
Richard Wagner's opera *Parsifal.*

On that full day, Plácido Domingo had performed an artistic feat requiring astonishing talent and musical knowledge. It had also been a demanding physical performance that few people could have accomplished. He had done what no other performer had ever done at that level of opera, which was the world's highest. If he had not earned a spot in *The Guinness Book of Records*, he had certainly gained a place in the annals of artistic endeavor. "It was all a coincidence," he said afterwards.[1]

It turned out that Domingo had signed a contract with the Metropolitan Opera to sing *Parsifal* a certain number of times and also to conduct *Madama Butterfly*. It was only discovered later that both operas were scheduled for the same day. No one would have blamed Domingo for backing out of *Madama Butterfly*. In fact, the Metropolitan's management offered to find a replacement for him, but he insisted on doing both operas. Of course, it would have been unthinkable for him not to sing *Parsifal*, for his performance in that role was one of the most eagerly awaited events of the season, and all his scheduled appearances had been sold out long in advance.

For anyone who was familiar with Domingo's career, it was not surprising that he did not hesitate to accept the challenge of appearing in both operas. After all, on a different occasion, he had gracefully met another difficult challenge. In September 1993,

Domingo had been rehearsing at the Metropolitan Opera in New York for the upcoming premiere of *Les Troyens (The Trojans),* a huge opera by the French composer Hector Berlioz. This was an important engagement, because it would be the first time that the complete opera had ever been performed at the Met. The opera was about the Trojan War (the war between ancient Greece and Troy) and its aftermath. It costarred the American soprano Jessye Norman in one of her rare appearances at the opera house. Domingo received a long-distance call from San Francisco. The tenor who was to sing in their opening-night performance of *Otello,* by the Italian composer Giuseppi Verdi, had become ill, and Domingo was the only tenor who could make up for the disappointment of the most important audience of the opera's season. Domingo rushed to the airport and boarded a jet that landed at the San Francisco airport at 9:30 that evening. He was rushed to the opera house by police escort and arrived at 10:00 P.M., two hours after the scheduled curtain time. He had put on his makeup on the plane and had just enough time to put on his costume and step onto the stage right on cue. *Otello* is a tragic drama of jealousy and betrayal based on the play *Othello* by William Shakespeare. It is also one of the most difficult and demanding roles in opera, and few tenors could have stepped into the role on such short notice, especially after a seven-hour plane trip.

Plácido Domingo uses his broad knowledge of music to take on the role of conductor.

Domingo performed splendidly, giving the audience much more than they had expected when they purchased their tickets. The next day he was back in New York, ready for his rehearsal for the opening of *Les Troyens*.

Perhaps a stronger reason for Domingo wanting to complete the two operas on April 22 was that it would be one more performance as a conductor at a major opera house to his credit. There are not too many first-rate opera conductors in the world, for obvious reasons. It takes a high level of musicianship to conduct an orchestra and direct singers at the same time. Also, it is a craft that is learned largely from experience, and few musicians have whole opera companies with whom to practice. Who would turn down a chance to conduct an opera at the Metropolitan Opera House? The chances are that Domingo would rather have cancelled his performance of *Parsifal* than miss his date with *Madama Butterfly*. Fortunately, the choice did not have to be made, and Plácido Domingo was able to add another triumph to his remarkable career. He had also put the musical world on notice that he considered conducting as important to him as singing and that his future career lay in that direction.

FROM ZARZUELA
TO OPERA

Plácido Domingo, Jr., was born in Madrid, Spain, on January 21, 1941. His parents were Plácido and Pepita Domingo. Both parents were musicians and singers. They already had made a name for themselves as performers in zarzuelas, which were the favorite musical entertainment for most Spaniards who lived in towns large enough to have a theater. A zarzuela is a play with spoken dialogue mixed with songs. It is much like an operetta or musical comedy.

Plácido Domingo, Sr., had a high baritone voice that would have been suitable for opera, but he chose to sing and perform in zarzuelas. Most of the lead parts in opera are taken by tenors, who have the highest adult male voices. Zarzuelas usually call for baritones, who have the next lower voices. Pepita Domingo was a soprano, which is the highest female voice and is given the most important parts in both zarzuelas and operas. She actually had a career in opera before she met her husband. She, too, chose zarzuelas over opera, perhaps because it meant that she could remain close to her husband throughout the many tours and hectic schedules of a performer's life.

There was no such thing as a season for zarzuelas. They were performed every day throughout the year, with matinees on Saturdays and sometimes three performances on Sundays. Plácido was nearly born onstage, since his mother continued to perform throughout her pregnancy. She went into labor at a theater and had to be rushed home to give birth to her son.

The Domingo family was a large and happy one, with many relatives and friends. This was fortunate for Plácido and his sister, Mari Pepa, who was born a year and a half after Plácido. Their parents' schedules often required them to go on tour for weeks and sometimes months. The children were usually left with their aunt—their mother's sister, Agustina Embil—who carefully supervised their behavior while they were growing up. Aunt Agustina remained close to the family throughout her life.

In 1946, the fortunes of the Domingo family changed completely. The zarzuela composer Federico Moreno Torroba, who was a good friend of the Domingos, decided to form his own zarzuela company. World War II had ended in 1945, and all restrictions and difficulties of travel had been eased. Moreno Torroba hoped to take his new company to Latin America, where he was sure an authentic Spanish zarzuela company would be a huge success. The Domingos were happy to join the company, and they left on a tour of Puerto Rico, Mexico, and Cuba that was to last for two years.

Plácido was not happy at being separated from his parents for so long, but he and his sister were left in the care of Aunt Agustina, who treated them as if they were her own children. Plácido was enrolled in school and soon became caught up in childhood activities. He was an active boy and developed a love for the game of soccer. He became so good at soccer that he began to have dreams of someday becoming a famous player.

Aunt Agustina, however, saw to it that he attended school, took his music lessons, and behaved properly while his parents were away.

The American tour of the Moreno Torroba zarzuela company was a great success. The Domingos had been especially impressed with Mexico and had made many friends there. When the company ended its tour in Havana, Cuba, Plácido, Sr., and Pepita decided to return to Mexico for a vacation before going home to Spain. While they were there, many people urged them to remain in the country and form their own zarzuela troupe. They were practically assured of success, and they were so in love with the country that they decided to stay and start their own company. It took them a while to establish themselves and their new company in Mexico, but once they felt secure, they sent for their children to join them. Aunt Agustina would accompany the children to Mexico.

In December 1948, the two children and their aunt boarded a ship for the month-long voyage. Plácido was delighted—not to be leaving Spain but to be spending a month aboard a huge ship with restaurants, orchestras, and games and movies for all the children on board. The ship made stops in Portugal, Venezuela, Puerto Rico, and Cuba.

The ship arrived in Veracruz, Mexico, on January 18, 1949, three days before Plácido's eighth birthday. His parents were so anxious to see him and his sister that they took a motorboat out to meet the ship while it was anchored in the harbor. It was a joyful reunion, and the Domingos were once again a complete family. They traveled by car to Mexico City, where they stayed with friends until an apartment was made ready for

Unlike his son, who became a superstar in the opera world, Plácido Domingo, Sr., chose to sing and perform in zarzuela rather than opera.

them. They eventually settled in this apartment in a very old and traditional building where Plácido was to remain until he was twenty-one years old.

Plácido and Mari Pepa were enrolled in the Windsor School, which was an American-run institution, but only until the end of the school year. Plácido was then enrolled in the Instituto Mexico, an all-boys school where he could receive a more traditional Spanish education. He did not learn much English at the Windsor School, but it was an introduction to a language that he would use more and more as he grew older.

Plácido loved his days at the Instituto Mexico because it gave him plenty of opportunity to play his favorite sport, soccer.[1] He later said that the two great ambitions of Spanish boys are to play professional soccer and to be bullfighters. When he was fourteen, Plácido had a chance at the second when he and a friend went to a small training ring for bullfighters to see how they would stand up to the bulls. The small and fairly harmless bull Plácido was given to handle promptly knocked him to the ground. Plácido decided to go back to playing soccer.

Plácido's parents' whole lives revolved around their family and their zarzuela company, so it was natural that Plácido would be drawn into their professional lives. He attended as many of their performances as he could and began to hang around backstage, where he came to know and be known by all of the performers and stagehands. Sometimes he would be called on to perform small tasks, such as placing the sheet music on the orchestra's music stands. His parents also performed with other companies and singing groups and even set up a musical contest for children. Plácido won easily, since he had been singing since he was old enough to talk, but he gave his prize, a soccer ball and some books, to another boy who was crying because he had not won.

Thanks to the example of his parents, Plácido was never shy about performing. He volunteered whenever anyone was needed to sing at school exercises or parties. His specialty was the popular song "Granada," which tells of the pleasures and beauties of a city in southern Spain. Plácido sang it so often that his friends called him "El Granado."

Plácido was learning a great deal about the music business by watching his parents and the other members of the zarzuela group. He attended rehearsals and saw how a production was put together. He learned that a performance did not consist of just a few actors speaking, singing, and dancing on stage. It also consisted of costumes, scenery, lighting, and even advertising and ticket-selling. He saw how his parents would peer through the curtains before every performance, counting how many people were in the audience. If the house was full, they were happy. If it was only half full or less, they were dejected. Yet they performed as naturally and as readily as always. Plácido learned at an early age that one always performed at his best, no matter what the circumstances.

This did not mean that Plácido's musical education was just a matter of chance. As soon as they were old enough, he and his sister were given piano lessons. Twice a week, after school, they went to the home of a gifted teacher, Manuel Barajas, who drilled them in the basics of music. Plácido showed real talent as a pianist, and his parents were delighted with his progress. As musical parents, they wanted their children to grow up with a love and appreciation of music. Their experience in the hard life and uncertainties of musical theater, however, made them uneasy about pushing Plácido into a theatrical musical career. If he was to become a musician, it would be better if he pursued a career in the concert hall than on the stage. Unfortunately, when Plácido was fourteen, Manuel Barajas died, and Plácido was left without a teacher. His parents decided to enroll him at the National Conservatory of Music rather than find another teacher. It was an important decision because, at the conservatory, Plácido had to attend a great many other classes in academic subjects, such as literature, history, and mathematics. His interest in the piano began to lessen. Instead of spending a solid hour every few days with his own private teacher, he would spend twenty minutes now and then with a different teacher. However, he did receive solid training in other aspects of music, such as harmony, which is the sounding of two or more tones to create a pleasant sound. He also studied musical composition and solfège (sight-singing). He could already sight-read scores for the piano, and now he was taught to sight-read for the voice, which is a far different thing. When you read a note in a piano score and strike the key on the piano that corresponds to that note, the piano sounds the note in the correct pitch, or high or low position on the musical scale. When you read a note in a vocal score, you must sound the correct pitch yourself. In other words, the singer is the instrument, and his or her own voice produces the correct sound. Both musical reading skills would be invaluable to Plácido in his later years.

Plácido made many new friends at the conservatory. One was Eduardo Mata, who was later to become a famous conductor of symphony orchestras. Eduardo was studying conducting, and Plácido would often sit in on the classes, which were given by the celebrated conductor Igor Markevich. He thus became familiar with symphonic music and aware of the difficulty in holding an orchestra together while playing a lengthy piece of music. He and Eduardo entertained themselves by playing four-hand pieces for the piano and even composing music together. Whether he was aware of it or not, Plácido was becoming a complete musician—performer, composer, and conductor.

Another new friend was Pepe Esteva, who also came from a musical family. His mother and father liked to give musical parties at which everyone was expected to contribute in some way. Plácido attended them regularly for almost three years. He sang whenever a voice was needed, but his main contribution was as a piano accompanist for soloists or as the piano part of a chamber music group. He played anything that was put before him and in this way learned a great deal about every kind of music. He later wrote that he "developed as a musician more through those weekly sessions than through any other activity of my early years."[2] Sometimes members of the Mexican National Opera attended these parties, and Plácido began to hear the gossip, the stories, the legends, and the traditions of grand opera.

The National Conservatory of Music attracted not only the finest musicians of Mexico but also of the whole world. Many international opera stars would stop by whenever they happened to be traveling in that part of the world. Some would come for coaching or further instruction and practice, and Plácido began to notice them and attend some of the opera classes in which they participated. He still thought of the zarzuela when he considered the musical theater, but the opera was beginning to interest him.

Plácido had never had any formal voice training. His parents had given him some casual instruction, but he had never studied with a teacher as he had for the piano. He auditioned for a few teachers, but none of them interested him enough to make him want to study with them. It seemed to him that they were more interested in how the voice worked than how it sounded, and he believed that they did not help his singing at all. Years later he was to find out that they may have been right and that he was wrong in not listening to them.

Plácido's transfer to the Conservatory of Music was a very important event in his young life. If his piano teacher had not died, he might have continued studying with the goal of becoming a concert pianist. Up until that time, he admitted later, he had nothing on his mind but soccer and the piano. The school he attended was strictly a boys' school, and he had had no experience with girls or women outside of his close-knit family. His upbringing had been supervised by a Spanish gentlewoman, his Aunt Agustina, who believed in a strict code of behavior.

At the conservatory, Domingo was suddenly thrown into a lively group of young people preparing themselves for careers in music. Boys and girls studied, performed, and socialized together within an atmosphere of freedom. Instead of going straight home from school or the soccer field, Domingo now would go to student gatherings or parties or would stay after school to practice piano or singing. He became very interested in a girl who would accompany him on the piano while he sang, and they began to see a lot of each other. He was only sixteen and she was a few years older, but he decided to leave home and live with her. The two stayed for a while with the girl's older brother and then were secretly married in 1957.

Domingo's parents were touring in Europe with a zarzuela company, but when they heard of the marriage, they hurried back to Mexico. They found Domingo and demanded that he return home with them. Domingo convinced them that his place was with his new wife, and they relented and let him return to her. Domingo and his wife moved into a new apartment, and the next year a son, Pepe, was born to them. Unfortunately, the marriage did not last much longer than a year. "It did not take us long to realize that the situation was completely impossible," Domingo said later.[3] They separated and were divorced a year later.

Domingo's marriage, the birth of his son, and his divorce meant the end of his education at the conservatory. He had to earn money to support his former wife and child, so he took any odd jobs he could find. Luckily, they all had something to do with music, so in a sense he was continuing his education in music. At first, he served as piano accompanist to his mother, who still occasionally sang at concerts. He also began to take part in his parents' zarzuela productions. He sang as a baritone so he could sing the leading parts. In opera, the tenor usually has the leading part, but in zarzuela it is the baritone who gets all the attention. This further convinced Domingo that his future lay in zarzuela, although many of his friends had urged him to consider opera. He had a high baritone voice that allowed him to sing tenor, and indeed one night he was called on to take the tenor part in a zarzuela when the company's regular tenor became ill. Tenor roles in zarzuela are as difficult as any in opera, but Domingo managed to perform his part without too much difficulty. It was his official debut as a tenor.

It was also while performing with his parents' company that he made his debut as a conductor. He knew the basics of conducting from having sat in on conducting classes at the conservatory. He was also familiar with many combinations of instruments from taking part in the musical parties given by the Esteva family. Since he was a singer himself and an experienced accompanist for other singers, he was certainly familiar with the special problems they might have with a piece of music. In many ways, he was the ideal conductor.

Domingo had not given up on his formal education, however, and he still attended or sat in on classes at the conservatory. There was one teacher, named

Although he experienced setbacks as a young man in Mexico, Plácido Domingo would later achieve success as a singer, actor, conductor, and artistic director.

Carlo Morelli, who impressed Domingo very much. He was a baritone from Chile who taught voice and coached many of Mexico's best-known singers. Morelli spent more time on interpretation of music than on how it was produced. He taught his students to go beyond the mere notes of a song or aria (a dramatic solo in opera) and to concentrate on its mood or feeling. It was in one of Morelli's classes that Domingo first reached a B-flat, which is a high note even for a tenor. It happened that the president of Mexico, Adolfo López Mateos, was visiting the class that day, so Domingo may have been inspired to do something special. He was very proud of his B-flat, and the road to becoming a tenor lay ahead.

Domingo was still eager for any kind of work—singing, playing the piano, or conducting. At that time, the popular musical play *My Fair Lady* was being presented throughout the world in every major language. When it was announced that a production was being planned for Mexico, Domingo was one of the hundreds of singers who tried out for a role in this important event. He was hired for only a minor role onstage but was also asked to be an assistant conductor and a singing coach. The play was performed every day of the week and twice on Sundays, and Domingo appeared in every one of the 185 performances. At the same time, he continued to accompany his singing friends when they found work in cafés or bars. Some of these jobs were in cabarets where the main attraction was the dancing girls who would follow their act. He and his partners were often told to hurry up and get off the stage so the real show could begin. It was a far cry from both *My Fair Lady* and the zarzuela.

After *My Fair Lady* closed, Domingo got a part in a new production of *The Merry Widow*, an operetta by Franz Lehár. It is still a very popular work with many fine solo numbers for the male singers. During the run of 170 performances, Domingo got to sing both of the male roles, one tenor, one baritone. It was not quite opera yet, but it was a step in that direction. After that, he appeared in another musical play, *The Redhead*, which was a detective story with songs. Domingo had now gained much experience in musical theater. He was ready for bigger things.

Domingo had a friend from the conservatory named Manuel Aguilar, whose father was an influential diplomat. Aguilar was one of the people who had been urging Domingo to turn to more serious musical theater. He now took it upon himself to arrange an audition for Domingo with the Mexican National Opera. Domingo agreed and prepared two baritone arias to sing for the judges. The judges were favorably impressed, but they told him that they thought his voice was better suited for tenor parts. When they asked him to sing some tenor arias for them, he had to admit that he did not know any, but that he would be willing to sight-read one for them. He was given an aria that he had never seen before and sang it through with hardly a flaw. The judges were so impressed that they offered him a contract on the spot—as a tenor!

At first, Domingo was used as a secondary singer in operas that featured renowned international singers. He also worked as a coach of other singers, which required that he learn the music from many other operas. His first important opera role came in September 1959 when he sang the part of Borsa in *Rigoletto*, by Giuseppi Verdi. *Rigoletto* is the tragic story of a court jester (clown) who plots against his master and in so doing causes the death of his own daughter. Borsa is a small part, but he appears on stage at the very opening of the opera accompanying the lead tenor. Domingo's parents were so proud and excited over his debut that they had some of their theater friends design a costume for him that outshone any on the crowded stage. When he made his entrance, many in the audience mistook him for the lead tenor.

During the 1960–61 season, Domingo had the opportunity to sing with renowned international stars, such as Giuseppi di Stefano, who was then considered one of the world's greatest tenors. Listening to Di Stefano, Domingo became aware that all he had read and heard about the great singers of the past could be accomplished by a living human being. He realized that greatness could be achieved in one's own time and place.

Another of his roles at the National Opera was that of the emperor in *Turandot*, by Giacomo Puccini. Although it is practically a nonsinging role, it gave him the chance to wear another magnificent costume. Domingo was not familiar with the music from this opera, which is the retelling of an ancient Chinese legend. One day as he was passing the rehearsal hall, he heard the chorus preparing *"Perchè tarda la luna? (Why does the moon delay?),"* and he was struck by its beauty. He later wrote:

> Perhaps if I were to hear them today, I would notice that the orchestra was playing flat or the chorus was not singing so well, but at that moment the music had the most profound effect on me. It was one of the most moving experiences of my life, the most beautiful thing I had ever heard.[4]

He had found his career.

FROM MEXICO
TO ISRAEL

Plácido Domingo made his debut as a lead tenor on May 19, 1961, in Monterrey, Mexico. The opera was *La traviata*, by Giuseppi Verdi, one of the most popular and beloved operas ever written. The production had been organized in Mexico City, but it was performed in Monterrey as part of the National Opera's second season, which featured mostly home-grown talent rather than international stars. Domingo was then twenty years old, and although he had already sung leading parts in zarzuela and secondary parts in musical comedy and opera, he was far from being a seasoned performer. He played the part of Alfredo, a lovesick young man whose beloved is a traviata, or wayward woman, in the language of the time. She spurns his love because she knows that she is about to die from a lingering illness. Domingo admits that the part of Alfredo is still a difficult one for him, and at the age of twenty, he had trouble controlling his emotion in the final scene when he sang, "No, you won't die," to the lead soprano, Violetta.

In the second act, Alfredo receives a letter from Violetta in which she tells him that their love is impossible and that she is leaving him. The letter is supposed to be delivered by a messenger, but unfortunately, on the night of Domingo's debut, the messenger did not show up on cue. After singing, "Who is there?" Domingo stood alone on stage, staring at the door through which the messenger was supposed to appear. What to do? "No one," Domingo sang in desperation. He then noticed that there were some papers left on the desk from the previous scene in which Violetta had written her letter. He picked one up, looked at it in surprise, and sang, "From Violetta!" and went on with the scene.[1] He may have been only twenty, but he already had the makings of a professional.

Singing in opera productions was not a full-time job, so Domingo continued to look for any work available. He found work playing piano for the Ballet Concierto de México. It was a touring company that could not afford to hire an orchestra wherever it played, so the music was provided by two pianos, one of which was played by Domingo. Again, he had to learn much new music and had to concentrate on his timing as some twenty or twenty-five dancers whirled onstage to the music he was playing.

At that time, Mexico's national television network introduced a cultural channel that needed experienced performers in the arts. Domingo was immediately available and soon had his own program. He introduced and performed works from the zarzuela, musical comedy, and opera. When he was not actually singing, he was either introducing guests or, if they were singers or dancers, accompanying them on the piano. His greatest task was to fill up the time with new and interesting guests, so he began hiring people he knew from his past at the conservatory and in the theater. He also had to arrange for the costumes, makeup, scenery or props, and anything else that was needed to fill up the small screen for the required number of hours he was on the air.

Mexico's cultural channel also presented many plays, and Domingo began appearing in them as an actor. He took his acting seriously and enrolled in acting classes where he studied the great classics of the stage. This training and experience began to show up in his operatic performances, and he soon became known as one of the few first-rate singer-actors on the stage. Domingo, as a musician, also planned the background music to be used in these dramatic productions on the cultural channel, so he again enlarged his knowledge of symphonic and dramatic music.

Domingo's divorce from his first wife had now become final. He was now able to lead a free private life. While he was attending the conservatory, he had become acquainted with a young singer named Marta Ornelas. They did not think too much of each other at the time. She was more advanced musically than Domingo. She had already sung in operas and was now seriously studying the great German composers, such as Franz Schubert and Johannes Brahms. Domingo was still interested mainly in French and Italian music for the theater and considered Marta too intellectual for him. Anyway, he was having a wonderful time performing in zarzuela, musical comedy, and television. He was dating another girl, Cristina, who sang in nightclubs, and to spend more time with her, he had begun accompanying her on the piano during her act. To Marta, he did not appear to be a very serious person.[2]

All of this changed when Marta observed Domingo in a rehearsal for *La traviata* at the National Opera. He was sharing the stage with the great international stars Anna Moffo, the soprano playing Violetta, and his idol Giuseppi di Stefano. Some of the secondary singers had failed to show up for one reason or another, so

Domingo sang their parts along with his own. Marta suddenly realized that here was a serious musician who knew the music perfectly and was not above singing the lesser parts when necessary. He probably could have sung the whole opera!

Domingo and Marta later sang together in an opera by a Mexican composer and were quite pleased with each other's performance. In fact, they began to see one another outside of the conservatory and the opera. Marta had seen Domingo on television and was very impressed with him. In fact, she secretly wished that she could appear on his television program herself, but Domingo never would have dreamed of asking her. He still thought that she looked down on him as a nightclub performer.[3]

Although Marta's respect for Domingo was growing, Marta's mother considered him something of a rowdy and disapproved of her daughter's interest in him. Domingo finally figured out a way of convincing Mrs. Ornelas that he was not such a worthless fellow and was serious about Marta. The Ornelas family was conservative and tried to follow Spanish traditions. One of these traditions that was dear to the heart of every Spaniard, and especially of every Spanish woman, was the serenade sung by the suitor under the window of his beloved. Corny? Not to Domingo. He hired a group of musicians, called a mariachi band, to play under Marta's window, with the understanding

Domingo's wife, Marta, goes over some musical scores with him for possible future performances. Although she was a talented musician herself, she would eventually retire as a singer to raise a family and help manage her husband's career.

that he would do the singing. The Ornelases lived on the third floor of an apartment building on a busy thoroughfare. After getting the wary musicians and their instruments through the street traffic and positioned under the apartment window, Domingo would give them the downbeat and then burst into song. Marta and her parents were charmed, but the neighbors were not. When they called the police, the police responded by asking them what they were complaining about. Didn't they know they were getting some first-class entertainment sung by a star from the National Opera? Domingo was careful to include some of Mrs. Ornelas's favorite songs in his serenade, and he eventually won her over.

Marta was having continuing success with her career at this time. In 1962, music critics voted her the best singer of the year after her success in the leading role in *Le nozze di Figaro (The Marriage of Figaro),* a comic opera by the Austrian composer Wolfgang Amadeus Mozart. Rather than let this go to her head, she continued to see and to practice with Domingo. She even gave him advice and coached him in his continuing efforts to make his singing better. She convinced him that he should begin to study the operas of Mozart and even got him a part in a production of another Mozart comic opera, *Così fan tutte (Women Are Like That).* In their relationship, Domingo was definitely the second lead, and their friends called him the

"Prince Consort," or wife of the queen. Domingo couldn't have cared less. He was happy for and proud of Marta and applauded her success. He was also grateful that she was helping him broaden his musical taste and style.

After the National Opera season ended, Domingo and Marta, together with a friend, the baritone Franco Iglesias, formed their own traveling opera company. Of course, this was a chamber opera, not a full company with chorus and orchestra. Domingo provided the music, playing the piano onstage, while Marta and Iglesias performed two small operas. The operas were both written for two characters, a soprano and a baritone, but afterward Domingo would join the others in a program of arias, duets, and trios from famous operas. The tour was a success, and Marta's parents began to look on Domingo with more respect.

Domingo asked Marta to marry him while they were on a trip to Acapulco, the Mexican summer resort. Marta wanted to marry him but felt that she could not do so without her parents' consent. The Ornelases realized that Marta's mind was made up as to whom she would marry, and they finally gave their consent. Domingo and Marta were married on August 1, 1962, and after a few days' honeymoon in Acapulco, they took up their careers again.

On the day before he was married, Domingo was pleased to learn that he had been awarded a scholarship for study abroad. He and Marta were trying to decide whether to go to Italy or New York to study when another friend of theirs, the Mexican-Jewish pianist José Kahn, told them there was an opening at the Hebrew National Opera in Tel Aviv, Israel. Domingo had always believed that experience was more valuable than classwork, and he decided on the position in Israel. What tipped the scales was the fact that there were also openings for a baritone and a soprano. This was exactly the makeup of their mini-opera company, and Domingo, his wife, and Franco Iglesias signed what they considered a "dream contract" for six months with the Hebrew National Opera, with a combined salary of a thousand pounds a month.[4]

Unfortunately, the money was to be paid in Israeli pounds rather than British pounds, which the Domingos thought they would receive. Israeli pounds were not worth nearly as much as British pounds, and it turned out that their actual salary would be $333 a month for both of them. Since they were both committed to sing ten times a month, this meant that they would be receiving the unbelievably low amount of $16.65 a performance. Domingo contacted the committee that had awarded him his scholarship and told them that he would need the money right away. They replied that he was no longer entitled to the award since he would be singing professionally and not studying.

Before leaving for Tel Aviv, the Domingos and Iglesias performed their chamber opera many times, and there were many other offers to sing in zarzuela and operetta, as well as their regular work with the National Opera. Unfortunately, Mrs. Ornelas died suddenly, and Marta was forced to cancel her engagements. Domingo continued touring with an international group of singers and also sang four performances of operas in the United States. He had made his United States debut in 1961 shortly after his first leading role in *La traviata.* He appeared with the Australian soprano Joan Sutherland in a production of *Lucia di Lammermoor,* by Gaetano Donizetti. He now had sung in Tampa, Florida; New Orleans, Louisiana; Fort Worth, Texas; and Hartford, Connecticut.

In Fort Worth, he appeared with the legendary soprano Lily Pons in *Lucia di Lammermoor,* and in Hartford, he played the second tenor in Verdi's *Otello,* with the famous tenor Mario del Monaco in the lead. By now, he had earned important credits and had appeared with many of the greatest international stars on stages in both Mexico and the United States. He was ready to step onto the international stage as a lead tenor and would seldom appear in a secondary part again.

FROM TEL AVIV TO NEW YORK

Plácido and Marta Domingo arrived in Tel Aviv
shortly before Christmas Day in 1962. It had
been a difficult journey in which their baggage, including their costumes, was delayed for weeks. On
December 29, Domingo made his Israel debut singing
the lead in *La Bohème*, by Giacomo Puccini. The
opera is about the lives and loves of struggling artists in
Paris and is one of the most popular operas ever written. Its opening scene takes place on Christmas Eve, so
the Domingos, in a way, had a belated holiday cele-
bration, even though Christmas is not celebrated in
Israel. Domingo had to perform in a borrowed costume.

The Hebrew National Opera was one of the youngest in the world and had no great experience and traditions of its own. It had to use many foreign secondary singers as well as stars in its productions, so it was truly an international opera. Domingo recalled a performance of *Don Giovanni*, by Mozart, in which the conductor was British and the cast consisted of two Mexicans (Marta Domingo and Franco Iglesias), a Spaniard (Domingo), a Japanese, a Greek, an Italian, and an African American. Rehearsal time was limited, and substitutions in casting were frequent, so sometimes the singers had to sing in their own languages. In one performance of *La traviata*, Domingo sang in Italian, the soprano in German, the baritone in Hungarian, and the chorus in Hebrew!

The Tel Aviv opera house was small and in bad condition. It was built by the sea, and sometimes during a storm, the waves would come all the way up to the theater. It was freezing in the winter and unbearably hot in the summer, and the air-conditioning would sometimes make the singers' throats dry. Rehearsals with an orchestra were rare, and there were no prompters concealed from the audience to cue the singers or help them remember their lines as there were in most major opera houses at that time. So the singers had to depend on their memories, their experience, and their ingenuity to get through a performance. "It was a trial by fire," Domingo later recalled, "and that,

In Tel Aviv, Israel, where Plácido and Marta Domingo worked
shortly after their marriage, the sea sometimes came up to the
front of the small opera house.

for me, was one of the most important aspects of the Tel Aviv experience. . . . Under those circumstances, I knew that I could sing anywhere."[1]

The Israeli audiences were enthusiastic and supportive. Even if the same opera were given fifty times a year, nearly every performance would be sold out. The local population came from every part of the world, but mostly from Europe with its great operatic traditions. They were knowledgeable and demanding, and any shortness in artistic quality was quickly noted by audiences and critics alike. This was very pleasing to the Domingos and their fellow artists, but it also meant that they were constantly in demand. During their first six months, Domingo performed forty-three times in four major operas: *La Bohème, La traviata, Madama Butterfly,* and *Faust.* He had performed the first three many times, but *Faust,* a French opera by Charles Gounod, was fairly new to him, and he did not have the usual time he took to prepare for a new role.

The opening night of *Faust,* which is about an old man who sells his soul to the devil and lives to regret it, was a success. Domingo was especially pleased because both he and Marta had done so well in an opera that was a first for both of them. During the second performance, however, Domingo's voice cracked twice at especially crucial points in the opera. Domingo felt terrible about it. He believed he had made a mess of the whole production and that he had placed a tremendous burden on his leading lady, who was Marta, and the other singers. The usually demanding audience and critics kindly overlooked what he felt was a disgrace, but he would not let it go. He went to the director of the opera, a stern taskmaster named Edis de Philippe, and told her he did not think he was good enough for the opera. She told him that this was non-sense, that one learned from mistakes, and that she had faith in him. All the other members of the com-pany backed her up, and Domingo later admitted that it "was the biggest boost anyone has ever given me."[2]

Marta, however, took the incident much more seri-ously than anyone else. "I'm glad that everyone else thinks your work is all right," she told Plácido, "but I love you and care very much about you, and I'm telling you that something is wrong."[3] What was wrong, they soon found out, was that Domingo had never learned to breathe properly while singing. Years before, at the conservatory, he had scorned those teachers who were more interested in how sound was produced than how expressive it was or how pure it sounded. Franco Iglesias, who was an excellent voice teacher, and Marta, who had had proper voice instruc-tion, decided that Domingo had to learn how to breathe all over again.

Most people, when preparing themselves for a dif-ficult task, breathe deeply, sucking in their stomachs and filling their lungs with air and then releasing it in a sudden explosion when they swing into action. Powerful singers, such as are required in opera, do the opposite. They breathe in by pushing out the diaphragm, the region below the chest, and slowly release the air from their lungs to vibrate their vocal cords and produce a sustained and voluminous sound. Opera singers do not need a microphone or any other electronic device to fill a huge space with the sound of their voices. If they did, they would not be opera singers.

Domingo and Iglesias devised a series of exercises for breath control and voice support that Domingo still uses and that have made him one of the most dependable singers in even the most exhausting roles. His voice has never been known to crack since, and he seldom needs to take a break or withdraw from a performance.

After six months with the Hebrew National Opera, Domingo and Marta were offered a new contract for a whole year, and their combined salary was raised to $550 a month. Despite the hectic schedules and the modest circumstances in which they lived, Domingo believed that his time spent in Israel was invaluable. For one thing, it plunged him directly into the world of international opera. He had to deal with and sing with leading singers from all over the world. He became aware of operatic traditions different from those of the Italian and French traditions in which he had worked for most of his brief career. For instance, the music of Wagner was not welcomed in Israel because of the association of his music with the anti-Semitic German Nazi regime. Also, the Catholic religion, which was taken for granted by the composers and singers of most of the operas in the international repertory, was virtually unknown to the many Jewish, Moslem, and Orthodox operatic personnel with whom he worked. Domingo had to broaden his outlook in order to work effectively with these diverse people. He never would have had to change at all if he had remained in Europe or America.

Israel also expanded his knowledge of languages, which is so important for any singer who wants to perform on the international stage. Up until his stay in Israel, he knew only a smattering of Italian outside of his native Spanish. In Israel, he had to learn Hebrew, of course, just to get along with day-to-day living, but he also had to learn how to speak as well as sing in the many languages of opera. This ability to understand and not just sing a language helped him immensely in his interpretations of the many dramatic roles he had to master. Once, when the tenor whom Madame de Philippe had hired to sing in *Carmen* turned out to be unsatisfactory, Domingo had to learn the part of Don José in French in three days.

Carmen is perhaps the most popular opera in the world. It is the story of a soldier, Don José, who falls in love with a fiery gypsy, Carmen. He deserts the army to be with her and then kills her out of jealousy when she leaves him for a bullfighter. Domingo played the part with such intensity that the soprano who sang Carmen, an American named Joann Grillo, was very impressed. When she returned to the United States, she told her agent about this wonderful tenor with whom she had sung in Israel. The agent arranged for two appearances by Domingo in the United States for the following summer of 1965.

Domingo and Marta decided that it was time for him to expand his range. By the end of their third year in Israel, he had sung in a total of 280 performances but in only ten operas. The Hebrew National Opera did not have the facilities or personnel for frequent new productions of unfamiliar or new operas. Once a production was ready, it was performed over and over again. This was not the ideal situation for a young singer on the way up, so Domingo decided to accept the offers from the United States and elsewhere. He did not want to leave Israel but believed that he could not make a long-term commitment. He proposed signing contracts for six-month periods, but the opera management turned him down. He would have to sing for a full season or not at all. Reluctantly, Domingo and Marta decided to leave Israel for the larger world of truly grand opera. Besides, they wanted to start a family. When they left Israel in June, Marta was pregnant, and she had decided that her future lay not in her own career but in her husband's and in raising a family. She decided to retire from the operatic and concert stages.

On the way back to America, Domingo and Marta stopped off in Spain to visit relatives. It was the first time he had visited the country of his birth since leaving it for Mexico in 1948, and he was deeply moved at seeing his homeland again. They flew to the United States, where Domingo appeared in *Samson and Delilah*, by the French composer Camille Saint-Saëns. This was one of the operas his new American agent had arranged for him. The opera, a retelling of the Bible story, had been written in French, but it was sung in English for this performance. Domingo was struggling with a cold as well as the new language, which he had barely learned how to pronounce. Things went better in Washington, D.C., where he sang in *Carmen*, the second opera for which he had signed up. He was such a success there that he received an offer from the New York City Opera to make his debut there in *Carmen*. His North American career now seemed to be well underway.

The Domingos returned to Mexico for a reunion with their families. While there, he appeared in a performance of *Tales of Hoffmann*, by the French composer Jacques Offenbach, and received one of the few bad reviews he has ever received. He was quite shaken by it and even had thoughts of challenging the

Plácido Domingo as Don José in *Carmen* by Georges Bizet.

critic in public. Fortunately, his agent called him in time to report that he had been invited to sing in Boston, in *La Bohème*, with the great soprano Renata Tibaldi. This made him feel better, and he decided to let the critic "live in peace," as he put it.[4]

His New York debut was scheduled for October 21, 1965. While he was rehearsing for *Carmen*, however, the tenor who was to sing in *Madama Butterfly* with the company on October 17 suddenly became ill. Domingo, who had sung the role many times and was conveniently on the premises, was asked to take over, so he made his debut earlier than anyone expected. So did his son, Plácido, who was born prematurely on October 21, the day that was supposed to be his father's debut in New York. Domingo sang that night in New York and then boarded a plane for Mexico to greet his newborn son. His New York appearances had been tremendously successful, but he was not on hand to appreciate his triumph. After a brief time with Marta and Placi, as they took to calling their son, Plácido fulfilled an engagement in Puebla, Mexico, to sing in *Madama Butterfly* with Montserrat Caballé, another international star from Spain. The next day he flew back to New York to complete his engagement there by singing in *Carmen*. Luckily for him, Marta was a woman of the theater, and she understood completely how important it was for Domingo to fulfill his commitments. Another wife and recent mother might have

Performing at the Metropolitan Opera House at Lincoln Center, New York City, was every singer's ambition. Plácido Domingo got his chance in 1968.

been upset by his leaving so soon, but she was not left alone. She had a wide network of family and friends, and she knew that Domingo was not leaving her and their son for selfish reasons. There was the audience to consider and his fellow artists and, finally, the music. She would not have had it any other way.

Domingo's success in New York led to many other engagements with the New York City Opera. Although this company always played in the shadow of the more famous Metropolitan Opera, it had earned itself an important place in New York's musical life. Its most important role was in introducing new singers and new operas to the world. The Metropolitan seldom took a chance on a new singer and a new or unfamiliar opera, but the City Opera regularly threw open its doors to anything that was new and exciting. When the City Opera moved from its old quarters in the City Center on 55th Street in Manhattan to its new and elegant surroundings in Lincoln Center, Domingo was chosen to sing in its first production. He was especially proud because the opera, *Don Rodrigo*, was a new work by the Argentine composer Alberto Ginastera and was written and sung in Spanish. The opera was about the life and death of a Spanish king, and everyone was happy that a Spanish singer would be singing the role. It was also the first time that Domingo had been involved in an opera from its beginning. He learned his role in the presence of the composer, director, designer, conductor, and all the other people who make up a first production of a completely new opera. Opening night was February 22, 1966, and it received worldwide coverage in the mass media as well as the musical press. For Domingo it was:

> . . . an unforgettable experience. . . . I did not fully realize at that moment what it all meant for my future. There I was, just a month after my twenty-fifth birthday and just eight months after leaving Tel Aviv, enjoying a great success in New York. It hardly seemed possible.[5]

For the rest of the year, Domingo continued to fulfill all commitments arranged by his agent and to accept guest appearances with orchestras. He made his operatic debuts in Boston and Chicago and also sang with those cities' symphony orchestras, two of the finest in the world. By this time, he and Marta had decided to make their base in New York, since it was central to his many engagements, which took him to Mexico and South America as well as to Europe. They bought a house in Teaneck, New Jersey, which is just a short distance from Manhattan. His family now included his son Pepe from his first marriage, and the house was always open to any of his numerous relatives who happened to be in the United States.

THE BIG THREE

In 1967, Domingo made his debut in Vienna, Austria, at the famous Staatsoper, or State Opera. It is one of the shrines of grand opera, and any true international star marks his debut there as a milestone in his career. Domingo sang the lead in *Don Carlos,* by Giuseppi Verdi, which was another tale of a Spanish king, although written and sung in Italian. Domingo had never sung the part before, so it was a double debut for him. There was time for only one rehearsal, and that took place in a rehearsal hall rather than on stage. Unfortunately, Domingo never got a look at the stage, which was tilted from the back to the front. When he came charging onstage for his first entrance, he nearly lost his balance and would have ended up in the orchestra pit if he hadn't caught himself. The words he was singing as he stumbled down the stage were, *"Io l'ho perduta* (I've lost her)," words that could also be translated "I've lost it," which he nearly did.

Shortly after that, he nearly lost much more—his voice. In January 1968, he was scheduled to sing two performances of *Lohengrin*, by Richard Wagner, in Hamburg, Germany. This was another opera connected with the Holy Grail legend, in which Domingo played the mysterious knight Lohengrin, the son of Parsifal. It was to be Domingo's first attempt at a Wagner opera, and he was so anxious about it that he spent long hours at the piano, practicing the difficult stretches of notes in the high-middle parts of the tenor voice that the role demanded. He also found the German language much more difficult to sing than the French and Italian he used most often, so he worked with a coach to learn the opera in its original language. Normally, he taught himself an opera by playing it through on the piano and singing only the main arias or some difficult or unusual part. For *Lohengrin*, he was practicing the whole opera, as well as singing in rehearsals.

Here, Domingo stars as the mysterious knight Lohengrin, in Richard Wagner's opera *Lohengrin*.

His first performance was successful despite a lapse of memory during an important aria in the first act. Domingo was very upset by his mistake and offered to withdraw from the next performance and forget about becoming a Heldentenor, a tenor who specializes in Wagner's operas. The audience and his fellow performers forgave him, however, and the reviewers overlooked it in praising his mellower sound, which was quite different from the booming voices they usually heard. He agreed to go through with the second performance, which went off perfectly, but the effort strained his voice.

Following his appearances in Hamburg, he had a busy schedule in the United States. Suddenly, and for no apparent reason, his voice began to break when it began a transition to a higher note. Everything else was all right, but a sudden change to a higher pitch continued to bother him. He believes that it was because of the enormous amount of time he had spent learning his *Lohengrin* part, with its long, sustained passages in the high-middle part of his voice. He became so concerned that he even consulted a throat specialist and had to cancel some of his engagements. Fortunately, the problem cleared itself up during an engagement in Vancouver, British Columbia, in which he sang in *Tosca*, by Giacomo Puccini. It was with some relief that he returned to his regular schedule. He was only twenty-seven years old, but he had already learned a valuable lesson—that his voice was not indestructible. From that day on, he always allowed himself plenty of time to prepare for a new or difficult engagement, whether on the concert or opera stage— and especially if it involved the music of Richard Wagner.

The most important event of that 1968, however, was his debut at the Metropolitan Opera in New York. He was already a regular performer at the New York City Opera's hall at Lincoln Center and was well aware of the giant new opera house across the plaza. It was every singer's ambition to perform in the new Met, and it was not long before Domingo had his chance. On the same day that he made his debut at the Vienna Staatsoper, he received an offer to sing at the Met. He accepted immediately, and his debut was scheduled for October 2, 1968, when he would sing in *Adriana Lecouvreur*, by Francesco Cilèa, an opera based on the life of a French actress during the time of the French Revolution. The title role would be sung by the famous soprano Renata Tebaldi.

When he returned to New York, Domingo continued with his New York City Opera assignments and at the same time took up his duties with the Met. As a rookie at the Met, he had to be ready in case of emergencies, such as a scheduled singer's sickness or absence, and to stand in for stars at rehearsals. Some afternoons he would finish a rehearsal or performance at the New York City Opera and then rush across the plaza to the Met to be prepared to step onstage if necessary. On Saturday, September 28, Domingo had just finished an exhausting week of work. On Wednesday, he had sung in *Il tabarro*, by Puccini, at the City Opera, and on Friday night in *Pagliacci*, by Ruggiero Leoncavallo. On Saturday, he was called by the Met to rehearse Puccini's *Turandot* with a new singer who might be called on to replace an ailing soprano. That afternoon he returned to Teaneck for a much-needed break with his family. Marta was expecting their second child, and his parents had come from Mexico to attend his forthcoming Met debut.

He intended to return to the Met to watch the last performance of *Adriana Lecouvreur* before his debut in it four nights later. He was shaving when he was called to the phone. It was the Met. In fact, it was the general manager of the Met, Rudolf Bing. "How to do you feel?" asked Mr. Bing.

"Very well, thank you," said Domingo.

"That's wonderful, because you are going to make your Metropolitan debut this evening."[1]

It seemed that for some reason the tenor scheduled to sing the part, Franco Corelli, had cancelled. It was 7:20 P.M., and Domingo had not planned to arrive for the beginning of the opera. Domingo and his father drove into New York, with Domingo warming up on the way. The curtain was held for twenty minutes, and when the stage manager went out front to announce that "a young singer" would replace Corelli, a ripple of excitement ran through the audience. They all knew that it must be Domingo, since he was to sing the part only four nights later, and that they were in for something special.

The whole evening was a tremendous success. Domingo had not had time to be nervous, so he sang easily and naturally. All the other members of the cast were rooting for him, especially Renata Tebaldi and the conductor, Fausto Cleva. There were not any critics in the audience, so everyone was relaxed. Later, when he made his scheduled debut, which was attended by all the major reviewers, he was calm and confident. All things considered, it was a pleasant and gratifying experience for everyone, except possibly Franco Corelli. Domingo later got to know Corelli well, but he was never able to discover the reason why he had cancelled his performance that night. Domingo had previously filled in for Corelli in New Orleans in *Andrea Chenier* in March 1966.

Shortly after Domingo's Met debut, on October 11, 1968, Marta gave birth to their second child, whom they named Alvaro. The following night he sang in *Pagliacci* at the New York City Opera. In this tale of the loves and betrayals of a group of circus performers, Domingo played the part of a clown. At one point he is supposed to throw candy to a chorus of children onstage, but instead the proud new papa threw cigars to the audience. The printed wrappers announced "It's a boy!"

Domingo's first Met season was supposed to consist of a light schedule of only two operas and an appearance at a special performance. On a Saturday afternoon, he was in the general manager's office discussing the possibility of his taking on another role. Franco Corelli had had to cancel that afternoon's performance of Puccini's *Tosca* because of illness in his family, and there was even some doubt that he would be able to sing in Verdi's *Il trovatore (The Troubadour)* in three weeks' time as scheduled. Domingo had just agreed to take over the role in *Il trovatore* if necessary when word came that the tenor who was filling in for Corelli that afternoon had become ill. Domingo knew the part in *Tosca* well and was able to step onto the stage at the Met after only a few minutes of warning. This performance was one of the regular Saturday afternoon Met radio broadcasts, and Domingo was heard by millions of listeners. Once again, Domingo had made a surprise debut.

Almost every opera singer's ambition is to sing Italian opera in Italy, the home of opera. Even with his performances at the Vienna Staatsoper and at the Met behind him, Domingo was still as nervous as any newcomer when he made his debut in Verona, Italy, in July 1969. He sang the role of Calif in Puccini's *Turandot*, which contains one of the most beautiful and difficult tenor arias in all of opera, *"Nessun dorma* (No one sleeps)." The opera also contains the chorus *"Perchè tarda la luna?* (Why does the moon delay?)"* that had so moved Domingo when he was still uncertain about following a career in opera. The opera was performed in the ancient Arena of Verona under an open sky. The moon was clearly visible from the stage, and the chorus to the moon took on an extra beauty and meaning. His costar Birgit Nilsson sang the part of the icy princess with such artistry and power that Domingo was "overwhelmed with admiration" and almost forgot to go on singing himself. He called this performance with Nilsson "one of the high points of my life."[2]

Domingo was received warmly by the audiences in Verona, but there was still nearby Milan to be faced. The La Scala Opera house is the most famous in the world, and *every* major singer since the time of Mozart in the eighteenth century has sung there. The audiences are the most knowledgeable and demanding that can be found anywhere and have been known to ruin a singer's career if they are displeased with a performance. Domingo had planned to make his debut there the following year, but he learned that the lead in La Scala's new production of Verdi's *Ernani* had become open. Although it is the title role, the tenor's part in the opera is considered small by many singing stars and is therefore shunned. Domingo did not feel

In December 1969, Plácido Domingo made his debut at La Scala Opera House in Milan, Italy, the most famous opera house in the world.

that way at all and sent a telegram to the general director that he was available if they needed an Ernani. A contract was sent to him immediately.

On December 7, 1969, Domingo made his debut at La Scala, playing the prince turned outlaw in *Ernani*. It was a momentous occasion for him, especially since his parents had flown from Mexico for the event, and Marta and the children were already there. He was especially thrilled to work with the famous La Scala chorus, each member of which was a fine singer in his or her own right. The performance went off beautifully, and the toughest opera audience in the world cheered him at the end. It was the holiday season in Milan, and the family spent the rest of their time there enjoying everything the city had to offer. It was a pleasant and restful time after his hectic schedule.

During the next year, Domingo fulfilled his commitments to the New York City Opera and sang his last performance there with Beverly Sills in *Roberto Devereaux*. This opera was Gaetano Donizetti's version of the love affair between Queen Elizabeth I of England and one of her courtiers. At one point, the queen (Sills) is supposed to slap her lover (Domingo), but the fake slap she gave him in rehearsal did not seem real enough and she was urged by the director to make it more believable. So during the actual performance, she really smacked him, and Domingo says he went on to sing better for it, but he was still a little put out. Beverly Sills went on to become the president of the New York City Opera Company and later the general manager of all of Lincoln Center. She is perhaps one of the most powerful women in opera.

At the end of 1970, Domingo had two engagements with the San Francisco Opera Company. When he arrived, he asked the general manager who the conductor would be. By this time, he was singing so many parts in so many cities around the world that he was not always certain with whom he would be appearing or who would be directing them. When he was told that "Maestro James Levine" would be conducting, his first reaction was, "Never heard of him."[3] Although Domingo himself was only twenty-nine years old, he could not believe his eyes when the twenty-seven-year-old conductor took the podium. The opera was *Tosca*, and it was Domingo's forty-eighth appearance in it and Levine's first. Yet Domingo realized immediately that he was in the hands of a master, a true maestro. Levine went on to become the principal conductor of the Metropolitan Opera and in 1975 became its musical director. Domingo has sung under his leadership more times than with any other conductor, and their partnership has become one of the most productive in the history of modern opera.

Domingo had now appeared in all of the major opera houses of the world except one—Covent Garden in London. If Milan was the mother of opera,

James Levine is the conductor and general manager of the Metropolitan Opera. Domingo has worked with him more than any other conductor.

London was the kindly uncle who took it under its wing. It had long been one of the great centers of musical culture. The great eighteenth-century German composer George Frideric Handel had been practically worshiped there, and Ludwig van Beethoven's great Ninth Symphony had been commissioned by a London musical society. It had its own operatic tradition dating back to the English composer Henry Purcell in the eighteenth century and had its modern genius in the composer Benjamin Britten. Domingo, because of his other commitments, did not make his debut there until 1970. Unfortunately, it was not the exciting, unexpected, and gratifying experience that his other major debuts in the great opera houses of the world had been.

The opera was Puccini's *Tosca*, the story of a tempestuous actress who "lives for art," as she sings in her famous aria *"Vissi d'arte."* When she learns that her lover has been executed despite her efforts to save him, she throws herself off the high walls of the Roman prison in which he was held. The soprano who was to sing the title role was Marie Collier, with whom Domingo had sung the same opera in Hamburg, Germany. In an odd coincidence, on the night before the opening, Marie Collier fell from the window of a building near London's Leicester Square and died. To add to the strangeness of the occurrence, at least for Domingo, he and Marta had just left a movie theater in Leicester Square a few minutes before her tragic fall.

Plácido Domingo debuted at the Royal Opera House at Covent Garden in London, England, in 1970. He had now performed in all of the major opera houses of the world.

The wonderful English soprano Gwyneth Jones had to take over the part on such short notice that she had to wear Collier's costumes. The performance seemed doomed, but Domingo and the cast gave it all they had in memory of Marie Collier, and the audience responded so long and loudly that the conductor at one point had to hold up the orchestra before resuming. The evening was a triumph, but it had an edge of sadness for everyone.

Domingo had now completed the grand slam of opera performance and was fully established as an international star of the first order. His future was assured, and he could go on singing in every major opera house in the world whenever he wanted and under any terms he wished. He could very well have become a male prima donna, traveling the world and accepting the flattery and applause of people from the very highest ranks of society, government, and the arts. Fortunately, he decided to try something new.

SHOW BUSINESS
AND MANAGEMENT

Domingo made his first recordings of opera in 1968, when he made two albums of popular operatic arias. His first recording of a complete opera was made in 1969, when he sang in Verdi's *Il trovatore*. Since then he has made more than two hundred recordings, including every major opera and such choral masterworks as Beethoven's Ninth Symphony and Verdi's *Requiem Mass*. Some works he has recorded more than once and at different stages in his career, so the whole range of his voice has been preserved for all time.

He has also recorded albums of nonoperatic music for a popular audience. Many opera singers have done this in the past, but none has ever had the success that Domingo had with his 1981 album *Perhaps Love*. In that two-million-album-seller, he joined in a duet with the popular singer John Denver for the title track and even sang a song by the popular English group, the Beatles. He has never considered that such music was beneath his talents. After all, he was the son of zarzuela singers and had made earlier appearances in musical comedy and operetta. He has made many recordings of the popular and traditional music of his native land, including *Music of My Country* (zarzuela songs, 1974), *Adora* (popular Mexican songs, 1982), and *Romanzas and Zarzuelas* (1986).

Domingo is also a fine actor, thanks to those many dramatic shows he did on Mexican television and the acting lessons he took early in his career. He is also striking looking—tall, dark, and fit. In short, he was a natural for the movies, and directors and producers were quick to notice it. He made his first movie in 1974, appearing as Lieutenant Pinkerton in *Madama Butterfly*. He recorded the soundtrack in Vienna in September and acted before the cameras in Berlin in December. In 1976, he made *Tosca* in Rome and remembers it best because his son Placi played the shepherd boy who has a nice little melody to sing at the beginning of the last act. His next film was the 1981 twin billing of *Cavalleria rusticana (Rustic Chivalry)* and *Pagliacci*, directed by Franco Zeffirelli. This was actually a simultaneous stage and film production at La Scala, but Zeffirelli decided that some exterior shots were necessary to give *Cavalleria* the realism that the story requires. After all, this tale of betrayal and death in a small Sicilian village was a fine example of the *verismo* (realism) movement in opera, so the whole cast flew to Sicily to do some of the outdoor scenes.

His next movie was a complete film project, *La traviata*, carried out in the huge studios at Cinecittà in Rome. Zeffirelli was again the director, and he decided after a few days of shooting that he had an important project on his hands, so he proceeded very slowly and carefully. This was all right for the movie people, but Domingo had engagements in England, Argentina, Austria, and Spain, which he managed to fulfill while the shooting went on in Rome without him. The effort was worth it, for Zeffirelli was so pleased with the results that he delayed the opening of the previous *Cavalleria-Pagliacci* film so he could release the bigger film *La traviata* in 1982.

La traviata established Domingo as a first-rate singer-actor, and he went on to make films of *Carmen* and *Otello*. One of the reasons for his success was that he was completely believable in any role he under-took. As Franco Zeffirelli later said in an interview on public television, "With all due respect [to other

Plácido Domingo played the dual roles of Canio/Pagliaccio in Franco Zeffirelli's film version of *I Pagliacci*.

tenors], tenors are not the idol that women dream about at night. . . . They do over Plácido Domingo."[1] Another reason is the fact that Domingo enjoys performing and likes to dress up in different outfits and do different things. In 1983, he appeared on a television show with Carol Burnett and, dressed in battered top hat and tails, brought the house down in a high-stepping version of "Stepping Out With My Baby."

Although he had great success in the field of popular entertainment, Domingo never forgot where his strength lay, and that was in grand opera. He now proceeded to take on the most difficult roles that a singer can attempt. The first of these was Verdi's *Otello*, which has long been a trial for many singers and has even ruined some voices. "The second act is like an opera in itself," Domingo has said, "the equal of *Pagliacci* maybe. . . . It is the most difficult act of any opera."[2] Most tenors do not undertake the role until late in their careers, after their voices have matured and have survived the strain of years of singing in all types of roles. Furthermore, the strain of singing *Otello* could somehow take the lightness out of a voice and make it unsuitable for lyric operas such as *La Bohème*. In fact, the German conductor and composer Rolf Liebermann said, when he learned of Domingo's decision to sing *Otello*, "Keep your ears open as you listen to Plácido, because this will probably be his last *Bohème*."[3]

Nevertheless, Domingo went ahead and performed in *Otello* on the night of September 28, 1975, when he was thirty-four years old. Domingo has said quite simply that he considers it one of the most important dates in his career. Not only was he a resounding success in the role, but, as he later wrote:

> It revealed to me a new way of singing that has made the rest of my repertoire much easier for me. . . . The vocal challenge taught me how to use my potential more fully, and the musical challenge helped me as an artist.[4]

From then on, critics were listening for flaws in Domingo's voice in other roles, eager to blame it on *Otello*, but none were heard. Even Liebermann had to admit that he was wrong. Since then, Domingo has sung *Otello* well over a hundred times, and he has become so identified with the role that many other tenors hesitate to take it on because they know they will be unfavorably compared to Domingo. As *The Times* of London put it, "Since Domingo first sang *Otello*, all other interpreters have appeared mere substitutes."[5] He later starred in a lavish movie version of the opera, directed by Franco Zeffirelli, which further fixed in the public's mind the image of Domingo as Shakespeare's tragic Moor of Venice.

Domingo has become known as a complete musician as much by accident as by choice. Since his first interest was the piano and he had seriously considered a career as a concert pianist, his ability to sight-read and analyze scores was with him from the beginning. At the conservatory, he had the chance to sit in on conducting classes and had stepped in when his parents needed a conductor for one of their zarzuelas. His evenings at the gatherings of the Esteva family in Mexico City, where he accompanied other artists on the piano and played with other musicians in complex chamber music, taught him how to balance different musical forces. He had also had experience in coaching both individual singers and choruses as part of his duties as a junior member of several opera companies. Due to his experience as a producer, director, and actor in television, he knew just about everything there was to know about putting a show together. It was natural for him, therefore, to look beyond his role in the musical world as a singer and performer. "Conducting has always been in my mind," he has said,[6] and now he began to think of conducting and directing as the end of all his experience and training.

In 1972, Domingo had made a recording with Sherrill Milnes, the American baritone with whom he had performed many times. Milnes had also had some experience conducting, so they teamed up in an album called *Domingo Conducts Milnes! Milnes Conducts Domingo!* in which they each conducted the orchestra while the other sang. Even though the orchestra was the excellent New Philharmonia Orchestra of London,

Film and stage director Franco Zeffirelli has worked with
Plácido Domingo in both movies and opera.

Domingo realized that the album was a gimmick. His intentions as a conductor were far more serious than making novelty recordings, so he resisted all offers to make any follow-ups to what could have been a popular and financially rewarding showcase for his talents. Instead, he bided his time until a more serious opportunity presented itself.

This was not long in coming. In 1973, when he was appearing at the Met, he was given the chance to conduct a New York City Opera production of *La traviata*. The featured singers were people with whom Domingo had appeared in the same opera, and the orchestra was one with which he had sung many times, so the evening was relaxed and friendly. Domingo was pleased that such an important event for him had turned out so well, and he was eager to do more conducting.

Many of his later appearances as a conductor have been last-minute arrangements resulting from emergencies or some other unexpected reason. There was, therefore, little time for rehearsal or polishing of the performances, but Domingo believed that he was improving and could do much better when he had an orchestra that he could conduct on a regular basis. He was particularly proud when the conductor Lorin Maazel invited him back, after he had conducted a rather shaky performance of Verdi's *La forza del destino (The Force of Destiny)*, to conduct the Vienna

Plácido Domingo (left) performs with fellow singer/conductor
Sherrill Milnes. Both Domingo and Milnes have conducted an
orchestra while the other has sung.

Staatsoper production of Johann Strauss's *Die Fledermaus (The Bat)*. Maazel assured him that since he was responsible for the whole Staatsoper company, he would not trust the job to "just anyone." Such an endorsement by such an eminent musician did a great deal for Domingo's confidence, and he went on to conduct orchestras whenever he had the chance. He made his conducting debut at the Met in New York in 1984 and has conducted at Covent Garden in London as well as at the Vienna Staatsoper.

In the 1980s, Domingo's career was in full swing, and he was appearing in every major opera house throughout the world. He was, as he told an interviewer, "living out of a suitcase," and he always regretted being separated from his family for long periods of time. Although he was living in the United States, he spent only a third of his time there. He and Marta decided to make Spain their permanent home, where they could keep in closer contact with family and personal and professional friends and still be close to the center of world musical activity. Added to this, of course, was his love for his native country and, especially, for the Spanish language. Having to work almost every day of his professional life speaking a variety of languages, his idea of real relaxation was to be among friends speaking Spanish. Also, he has always been intensely proud of the rich Spanish cultural tradition he has inherited, and he could be truly in touch with it in his native Spain.

He always enjoyed performing in Spain. At an outdoor concert in Madrid in 1982, a crowd of two hundred fifty thousand showed up. The sponsors of the concert had provided seating for twenty thousand and had allowed space for thirty thousand standees, just to be on the safe side. As it turned out, an extra two hundred thousand people had to stand for more than two hours to hear him sing.

The Domingos settled in Barcelona, Spain, but kept an apartment in New York City and a house in London, where Domingo's son by his first marriage, Pepe, now lived. In the summer of 1983, Domingo agreed to make a movie version of *Carmen*, which was to be filmed on location in Spain. Most of the shooting took place in the ancient city of Ronda in the province of Andalusia in southern Spain. The filming took several months to complete, and for Domingo, it was an extended vacation, the longest time he had spent in Spain since he was a child. He was joined by his sons and any relatives who happened to drop by. He was so pleased and entranced by Andalusia that he has expressed his desire to eventually make it his home.

Domingo's parents and most of his large extended family continued to reside in Mexico, and Marta still insists that they maintain a home in Acapulco where Domingo can relax, always knowing that the house will be filled with the family and friends he enjoys seeing so much.

In September 1985, Mexico City, the largest city in the world, was struck by a devastating earthquake. Whole sections of the city were destroyed, and thousands of people were trapped beneath the ruined buildings. Domingo was then appearing in Chicago with the Lyric Opera, and he immediately cancelled all his performances and rushed to Mexico City to search for his relatives and to do anything he could to help. He put on a hard hat and joined the rescue workers in digging through the rubble in search of survivors. Unfortunately, an aunt, an uncle, and two cousins had died in the disaster, together with seven thousand others. Domingo spent the rest of the year and the concert season giving concerts to raise money for relief of the earthquake victims.

The year 1992 was the five hundredth anniversary of Columbus's first voyage to the New World, and it was also the year that the International Olympic Summer Games were held in Barcelona. The city of Seville, about five hundred fifty miles southwest of Barcelona, decided to hold a world's fair as a cultural counterpart to the other two events. It was to be known as Expo '92, short for the 1992 Seville Universal Exposition, and an ambitious program of theatrical, musical, scientific, and technological displays was planned. To act as director of the many musical events, the directors chose Spain's most prominent musical personality, Plácido Domingo.

This was not the first time Domingo had been asked to become the director of a large musical undertaking. He had recently become musical advisor to the Los Angeles City Opera and was now doing similar work for the new opera house, the Maestranza, in Seville. As a result, he already knew a lot about getting large musical forces together and drawing on talent from all parts of the world. He had great plans for Expo '92, and he announced that they would take as their theme the city of Seville itself. He called attention to the fact that, although one does not think of Seville as a great operatic center, there are more operas written with Seville as a setting than any other city. Domingo said that there were more than eighty, but no one pressed him for a listing. Most famous are Gioacchino Rossini's *The Barber of Seville* and Mozart's *The Marriage of Figaro*, both of which use many of the same characters. Then there is Bizet's *Carmen*, with its grand scene outside the bullring in Seville, and Mozart's *Don Giovanni*, Verdi's *La forza del destino*, Beethoven's only opera, *Fidelio*, and many, many lesser works. Domingo's original plan was to have as many operas as possible performed in their original settings—*Carmen* in the grand Plaza de España, *The Barber of Seville* in the streets of Seville, *Don Giovanni* in a suburban mansion, and so on.

Unfortunately, he was limited to three operas because of the tremendous number of musicians and singers required, all from different international companies. So, on April 24, 1992, he opened the festivities by conducting the Gran Teatro de Liceo of Barcelona in an almost all-Spanish production of *Carmen*. The performance was held in the Maestranza, the theater Domingo had done much to promote and for which he served as musical advisor. The success of Expo '92 was due in large part to the dazzling musical program, which far outdid anything ever offered by previous world fairs.

Ever since his debut in Wagner's *Lohengrin*, which had so strained his voice that he had "three and a half horrible months"[7] recovering his voice and his confidence, Domingo had stayed away from Wagnerian roles. But now, with *Otello* behind him, he decided to become a Heldentenor, that special breed of singers who are able to perform adequately in the operas of Richard Wagner. In 1990, he recorded Wagner's *Tannhäuser*, the story of a minstrel who sins and then finds forgiveness through love before he dies. This is not one of the heavier Wagnerian roles, since there is a song contest and other episodes that call for a lyricism that is not too difficult for a tenor from the Italian and French traditions of opera. However, there are enough long difficult passages in the high-middle range of the voice to make it a true Heldentenor role.

In 1991, Domingo decided to take on one of the most difficult and demanding roles in all of Wagnerian opera, *Parsifal*. The story begins with the knight Parsifal as an innocent and untried youth and follows him throughout his quest for the Holy Grail. By the last act, he has become an older, wiser, and weary warrior who has come to the end of his journey. Not only is the role physically and vocally exhausting, but it requires great acting ability to make Parsifal believable, particularly in the beginning as a young man. Domingo decided to make his debut in the opera at the Metropolitan Opera House in New York. According to one critic, Domingo "put all his chips on an all-or-nothing roll."[8] There were rumors in the musical world that after working on the part for a while Domingo was beginning to doubt that he could bring it off. To anyone who knew Domingo's past record, this seemed unlikely. On the night of March 15, 1991, when the curtain rose on *Parsifal*, he was at center stage delivering, in the words of one critic, "the rich, powerful middle and lower tones that Mr. Domingo commanded all evening."[9]

Domingo has recently added another Wagnerian role to his repertory, that of Siegmund in *Die Walküre*. Again, he triumphed in the difficult role, adding:

Something valuable to it from Italian opera: a supple lyricism that can transform a Wagner role . . . into a character with some emotional depth.

. . . Mr. Domingo conveyed Siegmund's passion
and pain in a way that his predecessors . . . never
approached."[10]

Domingo was on his way to becoming not only one
of the greatest tenors who ever sang but also one of the
greatest Heldentenors.

With his increasing participation in the managerial
side of opera and his notable success in seeing Expo '92
through to its triumphant conclusion, Domingo has
become an important figure in the world of opera.
Most singers spend their entire careers doing just
that—singing—and then retire to become teachers or
coaches or to tend to their reputations through recordings. Very few have become real powers in the musical
field—managers, artistic directors, agents, and all the
other people who may never sing a note or put a foot
on the stage and yet control the whole business.
Singers come and go, but these people remain, quietly
seeing to it that the art continues and flourishes if possible. Most decisions on repertory, contracts, and even
the highest artistic aims of an opera company are
made by managers. The position is crucial to the success of a large opera company that employs many
people, and finding the right person for the job is a
serious problem.

When the manager of the Washington, D.C.,
Opera Company, Martin Feinstein, announced that he
would be retiring at the end of the 1995–96 season, it

came as no surprise to many opera insiders that the man named to succeed him was Plácido Domingo. Martin Feinstein had built the Washington Opera from a small repertory company with a budget of $2 million to a permanent company with a budget of $11.5 million. The company not only serves the needs of the nation's capital but now goes on tour. It has also become known as a major source of new opera, using much of its budget to commission new works. In 1986, Feinstein had made major news in the opera world by signing Plácido Domingo to sing the title role in the world premiere of Gian Carlo Menotti's opera *Goya*. Before that, Domingo had chosen the Washington Opera as one of the first companies to sing for after his return from Tel Aviv in 1965.

The Washington Opera is poised to become a major force in American opera, and the Domingos are determined to make it one of the great opera companies. Marta has said that all of her efforts from now on and as much time as Plácido can spare from his schedule will be devoted exclusively to the Washington Opera. "We don't stop talking about it all day long," she said in a television interview. "I think that at this very moment it is our only subject. . . . We are absolutely in love with this project."[11] Besides assisting her husband, Marta will become one of the company's stage directors. When asked if he would sing as well as conduct his own opera orchestra, Domingo said that he would sing at least one opera a season "if it's allowed."[12] It is hard to imagine anyone not allowing him to sing in his own opera house, which is now in the Kennedy Center for the Performing Arts.

In his new post as director of an opera company, Domingo will also have an ideal opportunity to achieve an objective that he has pursued almost from the beginning of his success—the discovery of new talent, especially Hispanic American singers.

He has always felt strongly about the apparent unawareness of Hispanic Americans of their rich cultural heritage, and he has done as much as he could to improve this situation by establishing singing competitions for young Hispanics. He believes that the large Spanish-speaking communities in the United States are being short-changed in what is offered to them as art and entertainment. He has said that many people are:

> . . . offended by what is presented to them and to the outside world as their cultural heritage: long-running television soap operas; brash, rhythmical music from the Caribbean; and not much else. This is hardly an adequate representation of such a rich multinational culture.[13]

One of Domingo's most recent best-selling albums is entitled *De Mi Alma Latina (From My Latin Soul)*, a collection of songs from all levels of Spanish culture.

THE THREE
TENORS

 For years, there has been an informal game among opera lovers to name the greatest tenor on the scene today. The game has become interesting because there are two who are very much in the public eye and seem to be natural rivals—Plácido Domingo and Luciano Pavarotti. Pavarotti had become a favorite of the public due to his open, cheerful personality, his impressive bulk which he carries unself-consciously, and his sheer showmanship. He specializes in roles that require a high, clear voice, and he was always willing to risk the high C's that the public

expected of a world-class tenor. It is no accident that his first album was called *King of the High C's.* There are no Otellos or Parsifals in his repertory, but he could always win standing ovations from his adoring fans in roles like Rodolfo in *La Bohème.*

When journalists began referring to a Pavarotti-Domingo rivalry, Domingo dismissed it as something that existed more in the minds of writers and fans than in those of the two tenors. In the 1980s, however, newspaper articles, television newscasts, and talk show hosts started referring routinely to Pavarotti as the "World's Number One Tenor," and Domingo decided to do something about it. He began to make more recordings and agreed to appear in advertisements for luxury products. Although he had often appeared on the cover of *Opera News,* he now began to appear on the covers of popular magazines, such as *Newsweek.* He dropped his dignified classical bearing and appeared in comic roles in television programs, such as the *Carol Burnett Show,* and even appeared onstage at the Radio City Music Hall with the Muppets' Miss Piggy.

Whether the rivalry between Pavarotti and Domingo was real or not, it generated a great deal of interest. Neither tenor spoke disrespectfully of the other nor criticized the other's singing nor did anything to turn the rivalry into a feud. Nevertheless, people love to know who is "number one" in anything, whether it is on the football field, in the movies, or on the operatic stage. Pavarotti and Domingo had never appeared together, and their fans were longing for them to face off against each other in a sort of operatic shootout. They got their wish, but it was far from being what they expected.

During the 1980s, another singer, José Carreras, had begun to appear as a possible third entry in the informal international rankings of tenors. Domingo admired Carreras, not only because he was a fellow Spaniard but also for "his courage in following his own path."[1] Unfortunately, in 1987, Carreras was stricken with leukemia, which nearly cost him his life. After a yearlong struggle against the disease, he made his comeback, and by 1990 was singing regularly again. The year 1990 was also the year of the World Cup soccer matches to be held in Rome, a huge event for Europeans and especially for soccer fans Pavarotti and Domingo. An enterprising Italian concert manager approached all three tenors, and they agreed to appear in a special concert to celebrate the soccer championship and to pay tribute to Carreras. They all donated their share of the proceeds from the concerts to charity.

The concert was held outdoors in the ancient Baths of Caracalla in Rome and attracted a crowd of eight thousand. This was hardly a record-breaker, but it became a worldwide event through television and a recording was made on the spot. The concert consisted of popular arias featuring each of the singers and selections from musical comedy and operetta with a few popular numbers. To everyone's amazement, the recording of the event became the all-time best-seller of any classical recording and earned millions of dollars for the record company. Although the singers did not share in any of the profits, they suddenly became famous throughout the world as "The Three Tenors," and one of the great acts of show business was born.

The next World Cup soccer matches were held in 1994, and for the first time, they were to be played in the United States. This would guarantee that the games would be watched by a television audience larger than any before. Another enterprising concert manager made an arrangement with the soccer authorities to provide the closing entertainment for the matches. He approached the three singers and arranged for a concert that was informally known as "The Return of the Three Tenors." This time, however, the singers were offered, and accepted, about $1 million apiece for their performances plus royalties on any recording. The concert took place in a sold-out Dodgers Stadium in Los Angeles on the evening of July 16, 1994, and was telecast to over one hundred countries around the world, viewed by an estimated 1.3 billion people. There had never been such a concert,

Plácido Domingo (left), José Carreras (center), and Luciano Pavarotti (right), perform together as "The Three Tenors."

and the recording that was made of it promptly became another international best-seller.

The next World Cup soccer matches are to take place in Paris in 1998, and already a "Three Tenors III" concert is being planned to close out the event. In the meantime, fans have seen them in concert at some of the largest outdoor arenas in the world in a four-continent tour. As a reporter for *The New York Times* put it, "The 'Three Tenors' phenomenon has become an indomitable force."[2]

On July 20, 1996, more than fifty thousand people crowded into Giants Stadium in East Rutherford, New

Jersey, to see and hear the three tenors in their only United States stop on the tour. The singers presented their tried-and-true program of popular operatic selections mixed with favorites from operetta and musical comedy. They even attempted an Italian- and Spanish-accented version of the popular song "New York, New York," the city's unofficial anthem. The crowd loved it. The event was also presented live on a pay-per-view telecast. As one observer noted: "The stadium crowd roared its approval, and so, I suspect, did viewers at home. . . . We got our money's worth."[3]

Near the end of 1996, Domingo had sung more than twenty-seven hundred performances in one hundred nine operatic roles. Each of these figures is an all-time world record.[4] On the night of November 9, 1996, Domingo passed another milestone in his career when he made his debut as artistic director of the Washington Opera. The opera performed that night was *Il Guarany*, by the Brazilian composer Antonio Carlos Gomes. This opera had been very popular at the end of the nineteenth century but had practically disappeared during the twentieth century. It is the story of the love between a chief of the Guarany Indians, Pery (sung by Domingo), and the daughter of a Portuguese nobleman. By reintroducing this opera to North American audiences, Domingo had shown that he intended to follow the Washington Opera's tradition of preserving old and nearly forgotten operas as well as performing brand new ones. It also showed that he would continue to expand the number of Hispanic works in the repertory, a mission that has always been close to his heart.

Whether Plácido Domingo continues in his career as opera superstar, conductor, or general manager, it is clear that he will not stand still. As a singer, he will continue exploring new roles, particularly in the operas of Richard Wagner. As a conductor, he will have the opportunity to explore the whole field of symphonic as well as operatic music and to commission and perform new or little known works. As an artistic director of an opera company, he has the once-in-a-lifetime chance to transform it into a great international institution. And as a Spanish-Mexican as well as a citizen of the world, he will always spread the Hispanic cultural heritage of which he is so proud.

"If you believe you are at the top," he has said, "there is no place to go but down, so I think that I am always on my way."[5]

CHRONOLOGY

1941—Plácido Domingo, Jr., is born on January 21 in Madrid, Spain.

1946—His parents move to Mexico to form their own zarzuela company.

1948—Domingo and his sister leave Spain to join their parents in Mexico.

1949—Domingo begins to study the piano in Mexico City.

1950—He transfers to the Conservatory of Music.

1957—He marries his first wife.

1958—His son Pepe is born.

1959—Domingo auditions for and begins singing with the Mexican National Opera. He is divorced from his first wife.

1961—He makes his debut in Monterrey, Mexico, singing Alfredo in Puccini's *La Bohème*, and his U.S. debut in Fort Worth, Texas.

1962—Domingo marries soprano Marta Ornelas and moves with her to Israel to sing with the Hebrew National Opera.

1965—He returns to the United States and makes his New York City Opera debut. His son Plácido is born.

1967—He makes his Vienna Staatsoper debut in Verdi's *Don Carlos*.

1968—He makes his Metropolitan Opera debut in Cilèa's *Adriana Lecouvreur*. His son Alvaro is born.

1969—He makes his debut at La Scala in Verdi's *Ernani*.

1971—He makes his Covent Garden debut in Verdi's *Tosca*.

1973—He makes his conducting debut at the New York City Opera with Verdi's *La traviata*.

1981—He records the *Perhaps Love* album, singing the title song with John Denver.

1982—Domingo makes his first opera film, *La traviata*, with Franco Zeffirelli directing.

1984—Domingo makes his conducting debut at the Metropolitan Opera with *La Bohème*.

1985—Earthquake strikes Mexico City, and Domingo joins in rescue work.

1990—Domingo sings with Luciano Pavarotti and José Carreras in "The Three Tenors" concert in Rome.

1991—He debuts in Wagner's *Parsifal* at the Metropolitan Opera.

1994—He appears with Pavarotti and Carreras in second "Three Tenors" concert, this time in Los Angeles. He is appointed general director of the Washington, D.C., Opera, effective 1996.

1995—He sings *Parsifal* and conducts Puccini's *Madama Butterfly* both in one day, April 22.

1996—He appears with Pavarotti and Carreras in Giants Stadium in East Rutherford, New Jersey, as part of the Three Tenors World Tour, before a crowd of more than fifty thousand. He makes his debut as artistic director of the Washington, D.C., Opera Company.

Chapter Notes

CHAPTER 1

1. David Daniel, "Domingo's Biathlon," *New York*, May 15, 1995, pp. 64–65.

CHAPTER 2

1. Rebecca Stefoff, *Plácido Domingo* (New York: Chelsea House, 1992), pp. 34–35.

2. Plácido Domingo, *My First Forty Years* (New York: Knopf, 1983), p. 19.

3. Ibid., p. 17.

4. Stefoff, p. 50.

CHAPTER 3

1. Plácido Domingo, *My First Forty Years* (New York: Knopf, 1983), pp. 3–4.

2. Ibid., p. 31.

3. Rebecca Stefoff, *Plácido Domingo* (New York: Chelsea House, 1992), p. 55.

4. Ibid., pp. 58–59.

CHAPTER 4

1. Plácido Domingo, *My First Forty Years* (New York: Knopf, 1983), p. 42.

2. Ibid., p. 46.

3. Ibid.

4. Ibid., p. 51.

5. Rebecca Stefoff, *Plácido Domingo* (New York: Chelsea House, 1992), p. 67.

CHAPTER 5

1. Plácido Domingo, *My First Forty Years* (New York: Knopf, 1983), p. 70.

2. Ibid., p. 77.

3. Ibid., p. 87.

CHAPTER 6

1. Franco Zeffirelli, interviewed during the "Plácido Domingo" segment of public television's *American Masters* series, broadcast June 28, 1994.

2. Plácido Domingo, in *A Year in the Life of Plácido Domingo*, directed by Revel Guest, Kultur International Films, 1984.

3. Rebecca Stefoff, *Plácido Domingo* (New York: Chelsea House, 1992), p. 78.

4. Plácido Domingo, *My First Forty Years* (New York: Knopf, 1983), p. 135.

5. *The Times* of London, quoted in *A Year in the Life of Plácido Domingo*, directed by Revel Guest, Kultur International Films, 1984.

6. Plácido Domingo, interviewed during the "Plácido Domingo" segment of public television's *American Masters* series, broadcast June 28, 1994.

7. Domingo, *My First Forty Years*, p. 68.

8. Jamie James, "Pilgrimage," *Opera News*, March 30, 1991, p. 34.

9. Donal Henahan, "New Staging of 'Parsifal,' Featuring Domingo," *The New York Times*, March 16, 1991, p. 13.

10. Allan Kozinn, "A 'Walküre' With Domingo at the Met," *The New York Times*, April 17, 1996, p. C11.

11. Marta Domingo, interviewed during the "Plácido Domingo" segment of public television's *American Masters* series, broadcast June 28, 1994.

12. *The New York Times*, June 29, 1994, p. C17.

13. Domingo, *My First Forty Years*, p. 201.

CHAPTER 7

1. Plácido Domingo, *My First Forty Years* (New York: Knopf, 1983), p. 207.

2. Ralph Blumenthal, "The Three Tenors Juggernaut," *The New York Times*, March 24, 1996, sec. 2, p. 1.

3. Jeremy Gerard, "Three Tenors in Concert," Reuters/*Variety*, July 21, 1996.

4. Allan Kozinn, "A High Voltage Dynamo Named Domingo," *The New York Times*, November 7, 1996, p. C17.

5. Plácido Domingo, in *A Year in the Life of Plácido Domingo*, directed by Revel Guest, Kultur International Films, 1984.

Glossary

aria—A melody, or "air," for solo voice, accompanied by an orchestra in an opera.

baritone—A male singer whose voice range is between tenor and bass.

bass—A singer whose voice can reach the lowest notes for an adult male.

Heldentenor—"Heroic tenor." A male singer with a strong and forceful tenor voice who can sing the roles in operas by Richard Wagner.

pitch—The position of a tone—whether high or low—on the musical scale.

repertoire—The list of roles, operas, songs, or pieces that a performer or company is prepared to perform.

solfège—A method of reading music by using the syllables *do, re, mi, fa, sol, la, ti, do* to represent the location of a note on the musical scale.

soprano—A singer whose voice can reach the highest notes for an adult female.

tenor—A singer whose voice can reach the highest notes for an adult male.

zarzuela—A form of musical theater that is native to Spain. It consists of spoken dialogue and sung arias and choruses and its stories can be tragic as well as comic.

FURTHER READING

Daniel, David. "Domingo's Biathlon." *New York,* May 15, 1995, 64–65.

Davis, Peter G. "25 Years at the Met." *New York,* September 13, 1993, 64.

Domingo, Plácido. *My First Forty Years.* New York: Knopf, 1983.

Freeman, John W. *The Metropolitan Opera Stories of the Great Operas.* New York: Norton, 1984.

James, Jamie. "Pilgrimage." *Opera News,* March 1991, 34–35.

Price, W. "Tale of Two Tenors." *Opera News,* September 1993, 8–9.

Savilla-Gonzaga, M. "Pied Piper of Seville." *Opera News,* May 1992, 8–11.

Snowman, Daniel. *The World of Plácido Domingo.* London: Bodley Head, 1985.

Stefoff, Rebecca. *Plácido Domingo.* New York: Chelsea House, 1992.

Swann, Annalynn. "Bravissimo, Domingo!" *Newsweek,* March 8, 1982, 56–60.

INDEX

H
Hebrew National Opera, 38, 41–43, 45, 47

L
La forza del destino (Verdi), 78, 83
La Scala Opera, Milan, 62–64, 72
Levine, James, 65
Lohengrin (Wagner), 55, 57, 84
Los Angeles City Opera, 83
Lucia di Lammermoor (Donizetti), 39

M
Madama Butterfly (Puccini), 6, 8, 11, 50, 71
Maestranza opera house, 83, 84
Merry Widow, The (Lehár), 27
Metropolitan Opera, 5, 8, 9, 11, 51, 52, 58–60, 61, 65, 80, 85
Mexican National opera, 21, 27, 29, 30, 33, 36
Mexico City earthquake, 82
Milnes, Sherrill, 76
Mozart, Wolfgang Amadeus, 36, 41, 83
My Fair Lady, 26, 27

N
National Conservatory of Music, Mexico, 19, 21, 22
New York City Opera, 48, 51–52, 58, 59, 60, 64, 65, 78
Ninth Symphony (Beethoven), 67, 70
Nozze de Figaro, Le (Mozart), 36, 83

O
Offenbach, Jacques, 48
Otello (Verdi), 9, 39, 72, 74–75, 84

P
Pagliacci (Leoncavallo), 59, 60, 72, 74
Parsifal (Wagner), 5, 6, 8, 11, 85
Pavarotti, Luciano, 89–90, 91
Perhaps Love (album), 71

Puccini, Giacomo, 6, 29, 40, 57, 59, 61, 67

R
Requiem Mass (Verdi), 70
Rigoletto (Verdi), 28
Roberto Devereaux (Donizetti), 64
Royal Opera House. *See* Covent Garden

S
Saint-Saëns, Camille, 48
Samson and Delilah (Saint-Saëns), 48
San Francisco Opera, 9, 65
Sills, Beverly, 64–65
Staatsoper. *See* Vienna State Opera

T
Tabarro, Il (Puccini), 59
Tales of Hoffmann (Offenbach), 48
Tannhäuser (Wagner), 84
Tel Aviv, Israel, 38, 39, 40, 41, 43, 52, 87
Tosca (Puccini), 57, 61, 65, 67, 71
Traviata, La (Verdi), 30-31, 33, 39, 72, 78
Trovatore, Il (Verdi), 61, 70
Troyens, Les (Berlioz), 9, 11
Turandot (Puccini), 29, 59, 61–62

V
Verdi, Giuseppi, 9, 28, 30, 39, 54, 61, 70, 74, 78, 83
Vienna State Opera, 54, 58, 61, 78–80

W
Wagner, Richard, 5, 46, 55, 58, 84, 95
Walküre, Die (Wagner), 85
Washington Opera, 86–87, 94
World Cup soccer matches, 91, 92, 93

Z
zarzuela, 12, 13, 71
Zeffirelli, Franco, 72–74, 75